KAYSERLING

Also by Alex Smith

The Appetites of Morning, the Languor of Afternoons

Alex Smith

KAYSERLING

To Tom & Joan,
with all good wishes,

Alex Smith

OVERSTEPS BOOKS

First published in 1997 by
Oversteps Books
Oversteps
Froude Road
Salcombe
TQ8 8LH

ISBN 0 9515513 8 8

Cover illustration and design by Ingrid Smith
Printed and bound by Pressgang Printers
Southey Lane, Sampford Courtenay EX20 2TE

Acknowledgements

Acknowledgements are due to the following publications in which some of these poems first appeared: 'The Bridport Prize' Anthology, Envoi, Kent & Sussex Poetry Competition Anthology, Modern Painters, Richmond Arts (Va.).
Part of *Inclusions* was broadcast on BBC Radio 3.

CONTENTS

The Insomnia of Count Kayserling

Aria with thirty variations

Aria   The landscape floods with sunlight, shines with green;
I toss the rough blankets aside.
Temples and arches beckon to the park.
My steps are soft in search of measured peace.

I   I am suffocated with yesterday's perfume
and alien faces!
Away with powdered wigs and guests!
They throttle and they twist
until I do not know my name!
Away with powdered wigs and guests!

II   Someone is banging pots in the kitchen.
Quiet with those pans downstairs!
It is their nightly humour; lords
of shadow, they have no mercy.

III   I place my hand upon the coverlet:
I know that I am awake; water...
maybe it is only thirst
that has awoken me.

IV   Shadows of sleep:
hills - undulating, smooth -
shroud hot and coarse blankets.
Peace, peace;   *(palindromic variation)*
blankets, coarse and hot, shroud
smooth, undulating hills:
sleep of shadows.

1

V   But shadows do not sleep:
they dance with flames in the fire,
stretch through the casement
with the sliding moon,
leap and exult over their captive.

VI   How the horse would amaze me, as a child.
The thrill of its muscles working
would obscure the visible autumn
crashing through the bracken
and the woods. But the scent from the paths -
leaf mulch and fruit mulch and woodsmoke -
would bring me back to home.

VII   I had no toys, my sisters would break them;
how the wooden soldiers would crunch and snap;
my sleepless nights - still they rise against them!
How little solace in a lady's lap!

VIII   The moon is greeted by a candle.
Kayserling shuffles to the music room,
tinkers with the harpsichord
- doesn't keep his servants long.

IX   Goldberg of the chiselled features
and melancholy eyes
plays tonight. He will sit
at the cembalo and petals
will bloom from his fingertips.
Their perfumes will lull me to rest.

X   The garden temples are pleasant and cool -
there I can sit and rest. Why hunt,
when I feel tired and my limbs ache?
The garden temples are secluded, away
from prying servants' eyes. I know
what they think of Goldberg.

The temple is good for music,
alfresco. Da Gamba this afternoon?
I'm too tired. I'll wait for Goldberg.

XI   Goldberg plays well, but he tinkers.
Petals droop and fall before
the bloom is full. Always
the promised phrase about to come,
a counterpoint to give me rest.
But I anticipate in vain, gaze
at the parterre through the window.
What shall Goldberg play?
I'll speak to Bach.

XII   Nature, that apportions all things well,
by strict division, weeps out my years.
I, who cannot now tell night from day,
unnatural am, and divide my hours
among false clocks that grin and chime.

XIII   The great voyage of carpet:
I pace and pace in my soft shoes
wearing life away. The household
is abed; I lie down only
to rise again. Do they sleep
in heaven? Do they sleep in death?

XIV   That which is unattainable
now falls before me:
brilliance of fingers
across the keyboard.
A steady left hand,
a rock solid bass
like the earth sleeping
in its depths,
      I do not possess.

XV And yet all is a question of timing -
footmen come and go
carriages arrive and depart
the cook is busy in the kitchens
and Goldberg, who has the measure
of music, is never late.

XVI Today I heard a sarabande
that wound me in its wisp of air,

the sound became a winding-sheet
and made me dream of dreamless sleep.

XVII I wish Goldberg would play an elegy,
grave yet free,
fine spun from the air
transcending formalities of the house,
or the stone precision of fountains -

any season is the season of death
I have learned that.

XVIII Landscapes fill with sunlight
a flute beckons
from the garden temple -
this is the measure
of Hymen, of hands
joined and glances exchanged,
the gossip of gardeners
but not the measure of rest.

XIX I, Count Carl Freiherr von Kayserling,
Ambassador of Russia to the Dresden Court,
have endured enough. I am tired
of all things German: German food,
German women, German landscapes.

4

I think of Russia's endless horizons
and inhuman skies; and yet it is home
with all the intimate sufferings of blood.
I tell myself: I travel home for rest.

(For variations XX to XXV, Count Kayserling returns to his
home in Russia on a visit.)

XX   Tomorrow I will ride around the estate.
The woods weep with autumn
as though all nature were filled with fatigue.
Shall I become a child again, riding back
riding back to lighted candles
and my mother at the window?

XXI   The hallway
                    not the balcony
is where I walk
                    at night,   *(triple counterpoint variation)*
consuming the gloom;
                    the air fills
the ancestral dark
                    with poisoned perfume.

XXII   The woods breathe, the buildings breathe,
the world was made for man.
I find my life in both,
the boy I was, the man I am.
Sunlight slants across the library floor;
I doze. A book falls from my lap
and startles me awake.
How gently the building breathes -
these are my years which pass,
sunlight and shadow, the proportions
of life. What, then, is my offence,
wherefore my violation?

XXIII   The guests have gone and servants are asleep.
The house breathes in silence -
a living and a holy silence,
the silence on the face of the deep.
This is the breath of generations,
their imperceptible presence. I will
allow the measure of my breath
to fall in with the measure of those
that have gone before.
No word shall be uttered.

XXIV   Kayserling turns and rolls his frame in bed;
Goldberg has gone home.
Groaning, the Count swings his feet
to the floor and slumps forward
on his knees. Rising slowly
he takes a candle to the next room.
He opens the harpsichord case
and strokes the surface of the keys.
"Silence", he says aloud, "silence".

XXV   Opening the casement I stand and view   *(cantilena)*
the same landscape that harboured me
as a boy; unnoticed, chromatic time
builds gradual manhood. We move
through chessboard light and shade,
through chequered sunlight. The cedar
spreads protective arms, cooling the heat
of June; from its shade dear faces stare,
noble, familiar heads, long since
returned to earth.
              Worried by day,
haunted by night I tread my own
staccato measure with some legato
relief. Autumn is legato...
delicate relief, richness without glare,
long shadows, ripeness and rest. I shall wait,
prepared, sustained in evening air.

6

XXVI   I have considered
                the filigree
                   of the melancholy flute -
          with dinner done,
                wine supplied
                   and maybe wigs askew,
          it reaches
                into my heart.

XXVII   The seasons are a fugue,
                what begins will come round again:
                   the dying youth greens the summer meadow
            but mid-seasons are indeterminate;   *(fughetta*
                November and the woodland birds   *variation)*
                  awake with April in their throats.

XXVIII   There are enough troubles without
          the business at Court; the old fatigue
          creeps back and I feel like a piece of rag.
          "Kayserling, Kayserling" I repeat to myself,
          without knowing why.
                          I nod at dinner
          and in company too. Let them snigger;
          at least they don't suspect me of intrigue -
          I'm not considered alert enough for that.

XXIX   That sarabande and its variations
          made me sleep. The boy Goldberg has done well.
          Such a soothing measure, it filled my mind
          with sunlit landscapes, arches and temples...

          When I awoke, it was already light;
          I must reward Bach generously.

XXX   Since I have been sleeping better I have
       given more attention to the ladies.
       One in particular is deserving
       of my notice and I will discover
       her attitude towards me. I wonder
       if my appearance is improved,
       my complexion more fresh? It could be so.

       Life at Court is not too bad; at my house
       cooking is better than at my mother's.
       And tonight we shall have music -
       I'll ask for one of my variations.

Aria da capo

       The landscape floods with sunlight, shines with green;
       the rough blankets are tossed aside.
       Temples and arches beckon to the park;
       he gently treads the steps of measured peace.
                    ...

The Music Lesson

after Vermeer

The long view:
incisions of steel cold light
glancing across
the Low Countries
dissect the room;

the veins of each marble tile
are picked out and spread
like rivers on a map.

She is trying the passage again,
the strain of concentration
visible in the tensions
of her neck and back.

Plucked notes of the virginal
consort with the table,
the chair and set jug,
become faint emissaries
of threatened fidelity.

Her reflection leans
slightly inward
in the tilted mirror.

The tutor is standing
dressed ready for outdoors
as though about to leave;
it is not his house
and he cannot stay long.

...

Lyric from Malory

Witch-doctor, shaman,
Merlin fossilises within the rock
clawing to achieve the simple air;

wrought by her own enchantment,
Morgan le Fay becomes the likeness of stone;
seek for signs, but do not trust what is there.

...

Albinoni: Adagio

Dazed by the wind, only the wind
The leaves flying, plunge
Allen Tate

The burnt-out library...
the blackened leaves turning
in the breeze, manuscript
pages softly lifted:
a cold fire of sodden
ash for the melodies
of men; tumbled folios
have become a tortured,
twisted staircase open
to the enemy sky -
the blackened day resumes.

The leaves flying... the scholar's
fingers frantic among
the debris, his wild eyes
peering through a pince-nez
in disbelief: music
has turned to ash and ash
to powder in his hands.
But a ground bass remains,
an organ continuo's
mournful tread: the bass line
of our inheritance.

(Dresden)

...

The Dumb Boy

Mallards crashland on the lake,
air and water splinter into light.
Willow and ash weave orchestral foliage
in the breeze.   His cheeks burn.

Angels of light dance in the trees,
a blackbird tunes his ear.

The gift of air.

He cups his hands.

He will tell the world.
        ...

Cathedral

And there is this fear: those aisles of arches
endlessly reaching and up-thrown
might catch our breath into the vastness
as though the clustered ancient stone
threatened to ask some question from the dark -
us, so suddenly shuttered from noon's glare -
so that being itself wavered
and we, too weak to resist,
might involuntarily step forward
to affirm and, powerless then,
with that huge embrace, that great call,
begin to merge.

...

On London Bridge

Spring sunlight settles over the river
and the landmark buildings;
what you sought for is here; forebodings,
ennui or joy; time alone is giver.

You receive. The pivot of time and place
turns to eclectic vision
however banal the scene.
You are afraid and you will fall from grace.

...

Egyptian Mummified Bodies

British Museum

Each finger is bound separately,
        the final wound of death
requiring such elaborate bandaging,
        and yet they appear ill at ease,
these figures humped or laid askew
        in their cabinets for display.

X-Rays tell of a skull detached,
        of teeth still in place, a dislocated foot
and somehow these accumulated facts
        dispel the mild shock of our first encounter;
we are interested in the resin used,
        fascinated by the embalming process.

Staring at a cloth-bound head we cannot
        comprehend the lurch of time that divides us:
this is the physical property of death
        free now from all ceremony and cult,
present in our present, claiming attention
        but ready, at a touch, to disintegrate.

We see painted on the mummy's case
        bright pictograms and hieroglyphs
illustrating domestic scenes: hunting,
        offerings to the gods, a funeral feast,
but no chamber of horrors, no mawkish
        confirmation of our grosser fantasies.

Far from their easy climate and clear skies,
        these special and much recorded dead
lie for our instruction; this museum
        has become our pyramid, stored
with treasure that we recognise as art,
        gilding our greyer dynasties.
        ...

15

London Perceived

*(A found poem from the London Notebooks of
Joseph Haydn, collected and edited by
H C Robbins Landon.)*

Behind the Lord Mayor there is another man who shouts out
all the toasts as loudly as he can; after each shout
come fanfares of trumpets and kettledrums. No toast
was more applauded than that of Mr Pitt.
The whole ceremony is worth seeing,
especially the procession up the Tems
from Guildhall to Westmynster.
                    In France
the girls are virtuous and the wives are whores;
in Holland the girls are whores and the wives are virtuous;
in England they stay proper all their lives.

If anybody steals £2 he is hanged; but if I trust
anybody with £2000, and he carries it off
to the devil, he is acquitted. Murder and forgery
cannot be pardoned; last year a clergyman was hanged
for the latter, even though the King himself
did all he could for him....
                    an Archbishop of London
asked Parliament to silence a preacher of the Moravian religion -
the Vice President answered that it could easily be done;
just make him a Bishop, and he will remain silent
the rest of his life.
                    Mr Antis, Bishop and a minor composer...

When Mr Fox was seeking votes, a citizen said
he would give him a rope instead of a vote. Fox answered
that he could not rob him of a family heirloom.

                    8 days
before Pentecost I heard 4,000 charity children
in St. Paul's Church sing... No music ever moved me so deeply
in my whole life as this devotional and innocent...

In the year 1791, 22 thousand persons died in London.

In solitude, too, there are divinely beautiful duties,
and to perform them in quiet is more than wealth.

On 5th Nov. the boys celebrate the day
on which the Guys set the town on fire.

The Prince of Wales' punch:
1 bottle champagne, 1 bottle Burgandy,

1 bottle rum, 10 lemons,
2 oranges, 1½ lbs of sugar.
When a Quaker goes to Court, he pays
the door-keeper to take off his hat for him,
for a Quaker takes his hat off to no one.
Anno 1791: the last great concert,
with 885 persons, was held in Westminster.

On 4th August 1791, I went to visit Herr Brassy,
the banker who lives in the country...
stayed there 5 weeks. I was very well entertained.
N.B.: Herr Brassy once cursed,
because he had had too easy a time in this world.

The Duke of Cumberland had to pay £25,000
in an adultery case.
                    Violin part. A work,
vocal part and violin part.
                    Madam Mara
was hissed at Oxford because she did not rise
from her seat during the Hallelujah Chorus.

Lord Clermont, when the King's health was drunk,
ordered the wind band to play the well-known song,
"God save the King" in the street during a wild snowstorm,
so madly do they drink in England.
                    On 5th Dec.,
the fog was so thick that you could have spread it on bread.

The Hospital was built 1762 -
there were 1500 patients, among them
300 sailors from the last naval battle.

Mister March is a dentist and dealer in wines
all at the same time: a man 84 years old,
keeps a very young mistress,
has a 9-year-old daughter
who plays the piano quite respectably.
I often ate at his house; as a dentist
he makes £2000 every year. He drags
himself around on two crutches,
or 2 wooden feet.

                    Ebb-tide and flood-tide
every 7 hours.

They perform the same abominable trash as at Sadlers Wells.
A fellow yelled an aria so horribly
and with such exaggerated grimaces
that I began to sweat all over.
N.B. He had to repeat the aria. *O che bestie!*

                    The *Entrepreneur* of the Haymarket Theatre
pays that miserable cur Taylor £21,000 sterling
every year for the expenses of the opera house.

Milord Chatam, brother of Minister Pitt,
was so drunk for 3 days
that he couldn't even sign his name, and thus
occasioned that Lord Howe couldn't leave London,
and together with the whole fleet couldn't sail away.

Lord Avington set it to music, but miserably;
I did it a bit better.

The man was named Lindley, organist, 25 years old;
his wife 18, with very good features -
but both of them stone-blind.
The old proverb, "Love is blind", does not apply here.
He was poor, but she brought him a dowry
of £20,000 sterling. Now
he doesn't play the organ any more.

             ...

At Hemmingford Abbots Church

(Following the 1000th year anniversary)

A thousand years in thy sight
are but as yesterday.

I bat an eyelid

and am still here
the church is still here

in the twinkling of an eye
a lifetime

in a thousand years
this scent of permanence

the coolness
of carved pews
and flagstones
shut against
the afternoon glare

stillness -
dust settling

the great clock heaves
              and stirs
gears up to strike

yews tremble
thicken
in the heat

the sky pours
its marble tracery
towards dusk

gravestones
rusty with lichen
lean
into eternity

    ...

Sutton Hoo

Raedwald's hall, his royalty
abundant in the finery
displayed: sceptre and helmet,
clasp and buckle, equipage
of kingship preserved within
the ribbed womb
of the burial chamber,
the gold and bronze glowing
secretly in the Suffolk earth.
But a burial without a body:
this ship of death
anchored to the time
of its launching
in the earth's belly
without a captain.
Ceremony and rite
lie in the locked ground,
though the mound,
prepared for long gestation,
fails to bring forth its king,
offering instead
these bright gifts from death.

...

St Simon and St Jude

Father, brother, common man,
unknowable; and the common task
tainted, unhallowed.
Curled shavings pile against the corner,
the wood now planed and joined.
Mother, Mother, what was it you knew?
Suffer my hand, suffer it to rest.
Must wisdom always give birth to pain?
For days we stare across the dusty hills,
saying nothing.

At sundown, the cedars on the horizon
are dark women lifting their arms,
receiving doves.

...

Ten Thousand Hands Clapping

It is not autumn.

Poplars shake in the late August wind,
their dark leaves twirling
against wash-day skies
that scud past, white clouds billowing;
and across the shimmering
light-splintered lake,
violins, their sound
high in the clear air.

Silent faces.

A silent film.

It is not autumn.
...

Materials

i
Iron

Black, dense and sullen
resisting
the November mist:
this boundary post
askew, flagging
the tilted landscape.
Embedded iron,
stanchion of civilities
that share a kinship
with an unremitting hardness
still: throng of spear and pike
abruptly threatening
on the rise, or,
unforgiving to the core,
ballista bolt
lodged deep within the spine.

ii
Wood

A darker wine.
The interval's silence
recalls the music
from the air;
the arc-lights' glare
reveals
plush of burgundy
glowing across
the cello
carefully laid to rest
by gentle hands,
     espressivo.

iii
Bronze

And there is this green
of Celtic twilight
come to permanent rest;
a green fire
over the escutcheon,
the sky's fire
caught among the shadows.
Each artefact glows
within the darkness
of the midden,
each light is hidden
by encroachments of moss.
Flame within earth-mound conserved,
a primal kindling preserved.

...

How the wall weathers the seasons

(a pastoral)

Spring

An expectant quiet. In the still air of dawn
      the garden and wood crouch by the wall.
Uneasy shift of blue and green
      spears through the leaden light.
 The wall appears to recede,
      refuses the light, takes colour
from the olive ground, adopts a reticence.
      Approaching the equinox, the year
begins to slacken its deathly grip.
      Here, the pagan would reveal signs.

Summer

The wall moves with the light,
      insistent in the glare,
its shifting texture a testimony
      of earth; terra, terra-cotta
in the sun. It then disappears, as if
      by deceit, absorbs sudden cloud change
and is lost among shadows of holly
      and oak: capricious harlequin,
reappearing elsewhere with loosening disguise,
      the wall moving with the light.

Autumn

Most fully itself: the glow of each brick
        is reflected among chrysanthemums;
sunlight steadies, mellows, invests each leaf
        with an aureole as garden and wall become one.
Here is a celebration of the porous:
        sunlight and rain soak into the brickwork,
are received into fibres of foliage.
        At night, as the soil blackens, garden
and wall again unify, with trailing ivy
        glistening emerald beneath the moon.

Winter

Hoar frost whiskers the upper surfaces,
        the white hairs bristling topmost bricks;
lower levels are festooned with black moss,
        are covered with its carpet mass of spores.
The garden is vitreous, crystalline,
        each twig and stem ready to snap,
the palace of frost about to shiver.
        The wall flakes easily; a piece detached
leaves a pink wound, raw and dry,
        as though blood flowed back to the heart.

...

Here

the intimate wind
lifts each tuft
of roadside grass

the frost also
is promiscuous
with its deathly kiss

here
is every place
blessed and cursed

a sparse row of trees
punctuates
the ploughed horizon

lapwings
rise and veer
float whitely across
brown furrows

the light is full
of blades flashing
about tumultuous cloud

here
defines the now
drawn suddenly small
beneath momentous skies

...

Trees in Mist

(Audley End Park)

Hanging in mist like a charcoal sketch,
just barely discernible until we came close

when seemingly faint shadows
suddenly took on huge dark forms,

massive and impenetrable.
Dripping through beech and plane, heavy moisture

fell with mild explosive force, emphasising
the quietness of the place; shrouded

and shadowy, we fell to quietness,
were drawn to an intimacy of cold

and damp and dark: a daytime nocturne
of black upon grey upon grey;

a mystery of winter trees, of giant trunks
ending like thin black bones of birds.

...

Part of a Roman Pitcher

Whether smashed over the good citizen's head
one drunken night, or left
merely for worms and the damp
to effect a silent breakage -
only this fragment remains.
Brushed, labelled and encased in glass,
it takes its place beside coins,
pieces of leather and tiles.
Part of a good day's work
for this spectacled pipe smoker,
who thrusts his hands in old coat pockets
and walks home through the rain
listening to the crowd's roar
in the amphitheatre, and dreams
of slim girls in white robes,
delicately pouring him wine.
His future is the past, research beginning
at a civilisation's end, and mild
domestic rancour a small annoyance:
nothing so uncivilised as a jug at his head.

...

Italian Garden

That most of the gods are not genuine
      does not matter (most are fractured and some
lie face down in the tall grass, barely visible);
      it does not matter that some are copies
for all mingle in this gentle dilapidation
      marked by sparrows hopping across the dry fountain
and weeds spreading from cracks in the patio.
      The gods were placed in aesthetic contrast
to the trees and shrubs that have now out-weathered them,
      yet both share an atmosphere of desertion,
an incipient wildness whose encroachment
      is tentative. Neglect sketches
its own version of elegance: the rusting
      of the iron balustrade, the paint flaking
from the back of the house. But not all
      of the gods have deserted, for the sun,
possessor of the Mediterranean,
      is guardian still, definer of angle and edge,
discriminator of wall surfaces and roofs,
      impervious to history.

      ...

Survivors

Half-a-dozen women
are walking their dogs
in the freezing park;

snuggled in fox-furs
they step out stiffly
and stand like the charcoal trees,
brittle and age-gaunt.

None speak or make gesture
of acknowledgement,
having perfected
an imperious solitude,
a Habsburg delicacy filled
with meaningless protocol.

They inhabit a world
of faint tinkling sounds,
a distant music of tiny bells
silvered in the frost.

The years grind slowly
like a rusting, run-down
wiener waltzer.

...

Parkring, Vienna

What has the world given me but this swaying of grass?

A thin blue line, a horizon of thread.
Cities of glass, azure reflected upon azure, a world of straight lines
and right angles where the visitor is lost in a maze of double images,
where
a perpetual and unnerving silence is preserved and where the buildings,
constructed of mirrors, reach to the clouds.

Cathedrals of crystal. Baroque foundations of opal and quartz, colonnades
of jade, columns of convoluted ivory, sunburst through ancient arcades,
long shadows across marble floors, silent chapels...

and palaces filled with choirs, tier upon tier of sopranos, their voices rising
pure and clear in the dawn air; great halls, courtyards and domes filled
with celestial harmony, guiding the silent pathways of migrating birds.

And what else has the world given but this swaying of grass?

Seas, vast oceans of the deepest blue, the mass of ocean's undertow where
giant silvery fish gather among the rays of filtered sunlight to sing
motets and antiphons of Josquin Desprez.

And the swaying of grass...

the free abandon of gentle rain, the green haze of valleys, the grass
swaying in wind, the countless roots of childhood...

what else has the world given me?

...

Variations on a Theme of Marvell

Annihilating all that's made
To a green Thought in a green Shade

i

The strident macaw, raucous in the shrubbery, blazes among laurels. It
lives for the grand flourish, parading fierce heraldry in what it believes to
be Parrot Hollywood, perfect background for screeching razzmatazz, full
of exotic garden green.

ii

But what of Cambridge, stately sweet, where walls speak of history and
academics sweep bat-like along the backs? With what bold insouciance
purple and white crocus spear through soil.
Or Oxford, where clerics cluster in a hooded huddle, deliberating mischief,
tampering with the mysteries of tea-time, conscious only of spires spearing
the summer skies of blue?

iii

Purity will demand such forms.
But what of her in solitude, standing with wrists plunged deep in a bowl of
tepid water, her mind wandering as she stares through the kitchen
window?
The garden and the birds are one: apple boughs offer their gnarled wave at
finches descending from their element of green: delicate messengers of
change.

iv

Like is attracted to like: rain shrouds the hills, green veiling green. Spring
is evanescent, grey, carrying lightly its burden of returning song. A heavier
green is promised for later on, like changes in weather, but first we must
expurgate the deaths of winter.

...

Fountain

curvature of the green
rain-dashed morning

unbroken continuum
of spray parabola

lyre
of weeping
　...

Florence

Cold Spring

forsythia splashes
greening avenues and gardens
daffodils gather
in groups of heralds

but the wind
will have none of it

tearing clouds to ribbons
it lifts rooks
onto thermal lanes
articulates
their sweep and ride

the caul of sky darkens
threatens oblivion

and the moon
cold sister of women
rises
trailing her oceans

bloodless ghost
drained utterly white

...

High Raise

Langdales

A dominance of grey.
Red disk of sun, collage-stuck
into the west, drains colour
from every rock, each blade of grass.

Rocks blend with craggy
promontories of clouds:
rock-haze, panoramic
before High Raise.

And what should be said
of the slow wind that moans
ruffling the grass in rivulets?
That while all else moves, centres hold.

High White Stones, plateau summit,
summum bonum
of airy gyres,
boon of grace.

It is the foolish man
that asks for bread;
the empty man asks
a stone for his cairn.

Can shores exchange,
do continents shift?
Wind is master only
of the fickle, its drift

diverted by centres.
And what of time, erosion?
Our descending figures are specks
diminished in the salmon dusk.

...

Pre-Raphaelite Poem

Pegwell Bay, after William Dyce

The green lantern of twilight has dipped into the sea
and the grey cliffs stare full of ancient faces
among the wrinkles and crevices. Low tide.
Rocks, exposed in the shallows, recede into darkness.
On the shore, wife and second sister are intent
upon searching among the rock pools and shingle;
garrulous and homely, preservers of memories,
the perfect players of the finite role
from whom no mystery is inviolable;
wife and second sister, gatherers of seaweed,
shells and odd-coloured stones... dregs of a day's excursion.

But my silent sister, pale and wistful, stands apart.
Against that sea of gold-spun silk she seems
absorbed by some far away point as though
she had been waiting there for years -
the whole of our childhood suspended there
in the dark eyes of that Penelope!

The day, nearly over, is dressed in all
 its translucent finery and each of us
is engaged according to temperament
(the games are over; my son, tired, drags his spade
behind him) - and suddenly I am afraid:
what would happen if the impending darkness
claimed my silent sister, should close around her
and embrace that pale form, which even now
is merging with the gaunt cliff's shadow?

   ...

The Madness of my Sister

The greengages turn to ice
in the conservatory; soon
they will be pure light.

Sun-rays yellow the panes.
Two o'clock.
Afternoons fall away like pearls
sliding off a broken string.

The endlessness of detail -
always to waste time...
I haven't washed my hair in weeks.

Another dress to put on,
another demand.
Whose body do I inhabit?

How quietly I am vanishing!

...

Inclusions

I

I remember him tall awkward
with a young face so earnest but so young
and I as young and awkward
felt my world lift in those restricted embraces
I have never known happiness like that
tea was held in the garden on a Sunday
(those long hot summers before the war)
and in the evening's cool I envied not
those pale flowers their singular beauty
and in the mornings I would rise early
and stand alone in the garden and recall
his voice and his nervous look at my father
and hear again the plates being cleared away
male conversation and the lighting of cigars -
I remember
when hot and disturbed he gave me security
his hands were a comfort
for he was so beautiful

II

a place without friends
the bullets in rows
the rows in boxes
the boxes in rows
the rows on benches
the benches in rows
and us girls in rows at the benches
many faces and much talk
but I was frightened of their scorn
some words I didn't understand
and went home hating them after they said
he wouldn't be back their men weren't back
try your luck with another at home
they said and it hurt me in my groin to hear it
at home mother was silent
and I so tired after the factory

41

I would dream of death in a foreign country
and in the mornings I would rise early
and stand alone in the garden and recall
his voice

III

a man I know not queued for dole
and I bought bread for him and children I knew not
the furniture was foreign (being his mother's)
and I seldom ventured into the street
the children were strangers
but I was frightened of their scorn
some words I didn't understand
and went home hating them after they said
he wouldn't be back
but in the mornings I was sick
and if he came back
and if he knew -
the children talk so -
he would beat me
I wait for darkness and for sleep
so I may partially hide

IV

at fifty I feel nothing
save an ache in my bones
I sit alone and wait for nothing
in the park where I walk
they are piling up sandbags
I go back and listen to the wireless
and do not understand -
I know that Munich must be important -
but what is it to me?
nobody holds my hand
as I cry sometimes into the night
but sometimes in the evening's cool
I envy those pale flowers their singular beauty
and in the garden I recall
his voice and his nervous look at my father
and hear again the plates being cleared away

male conversation and the lighting of cigars
I remember
when hot and disturbed he gave me security
his hands were a comfort
for he was so beautiful

...

For Miles

(a found poem)

walkin'
I thought about you
in a silent way -
        all blues
        all of you
yesterdays -
        tempus fugit
               so what
               the theme
               changes
spring is here
blue haze
        blue in green
               no blues
godchild
pan piper
will o'the wisp....
        miles
               freedom jazz dance
               seven steps to heaven
agitation
        shhh/*peaceful*
               it gets better
in your own sweet way
when lights are low
        round 'bout midnight
               but not for me;
               enigma:
something I dreamed last night -
footprints, sanctuary:
        blue room,
        whispering
               it never entered my mind
miles ahead
my old flame
        down country son
               black comedy
my man's gone now

Alfred Wallis in Heaven

"Alfred   Wallis
Artist & Mariner

1855   aug18   aug29   1942

INTO THY HANDS O LORD"

here are things what used to Bee
great sailin ships glidin through
oceans of eternal blue
or ridin steeply hevens waves
under fast fairwether clouds
or them steamers cuttin strait
ploughin with the force of iron
then of a sudden tiltin up
and veerin hard at each waves roll
lurchin to the suck and swirl
before settin back to rights again
alls come right and strait again
no need to paint on cardboard now
to record things what used to Bee
to save aught from oblivion
here i have my company
of them who without talkin know
alls come right and strait for me
i tell them
i was Born in Devenport
Born on the day of the fall
of Serveserpool Rushan War

        ...

45

Sufficiency - a letter

"... room is reasonable. I have brought about 100 books with me...
adequate housing for them.... I'm situated on the upstairs storey of a
terraced row. From my window I have a marvellous view of the town and
the countryside - and the sea (just)."

R.C.

You awake to the chirping of sparrows
    in the gutter and rise to view
the haphazard tiers of houses, their roofs
    russet in autumn sunlight.
Beyond, flaring upland and copse
    consume the night's dew. There is silence:
the down-enfolded town, huddled against
    the stirrings of a cold season,
re-enacts the rituals of clarity,
    crouches beneath the swirl and screw
of tumbling landscape ablaze with bracken.
    And just in view there is the sea:
not the massive heave and pull of ocean
    but a twinkling slip of azure
caught between a near roof and a far field,
    reminding the eye of distance.
Distance! In the room are a hundred books
    (the sufficiency of numbers!)
and, arranged in their adequate housing,
    present the distances of time.
Then let sufficiency reside here - not
    in the glare of the failing year -
but in a glimpse of the secluded sea,
    for there change and sufficiency
must unify within the promised day,
    must hold within the ocean's sway.
    ...

Notes

The Insomnia of Count Kayserling

Count Carl Freiherr von Kayserling, Russian Ambassador to the Dresden Court, suffered from insomnia and used to have Johann Theophilus Goldberg play to him on the harpsichord at night. Goldberg, who was a pupil of Bach, did not always succeed in soothing the Count with his improvisations. Kayserling therefore requested Bach to write something for Goldberg which would have a tranquillising effect upon his nerves. This work, known as The Goldberg Variations, was published in 1742.

What has the world given me but this swaying of grass

The title is taken from Anabasis by St. - J. Perse, translated by T. S. Eliot: *Que m'a donne le monde que ce mouvement d'herbes?* (part VIII).

For Miles

The poem is made up of titles taken from Miles Davis's recordings.

Alfred Wallis in Heaven

The epigraph is taken from Alfred Wallis's grave in St. Ives, Cornwall.
The spelling used in the poem is taken as closely as possible from that used in Wallis's own correspondence. The last three lines are from a letter from Wallis to H. S. Ede, 6 April 1935.